Free Verse Editions

Edited by Jon Thompson

General Release from the Beginning of the World

Donna Spruijt-Metz

Parlor Press
Anderson, South Carolina
www.parlorpress.com

Parlor Press LLC, Anderson, South Carolina, 29621

Library of Congress Cataloging-in-Publication Data on File

978-1-64317-351-1 (paperback)
978-1-64317-352-8 (PDF)
978-1-64317-353-5 (EPUB)

1 2 3 4 5

Cover art: Grapes on a String by Gershom, oil on panel. Used by permission.
Cover design by David Blakesley.

Parlor Press, LLC is an independent publisher of scholarly and trade titles in print
and multimedia formats. This book is available in paperback and ebook formats
from Parlor Press on the World Wide Web at https://parlorpress.com or through
online and brick-and-mortar bookstores. For submission information or to find
out about Parlor Press publications, write to Parlor Press, 3015 Brackenberry
Drive, Anderson, South Carolina, 29621, or email editor@parlorpress.com.

Within

Contents

If we can make, from tenderness, a revolution—

—Carl Phillips

I Need the Long March

When I was my grandmother's mother I knew
she would be beautiful in the time of war
so I set to knitting her

a whole skein of swans
in flawless V formation

pearl-colored
to match her skin,
steadfast guides for the long march

I sewed coins and jewelry into the hem of her dress
copal, charms, carnelian and ash
into her long sleeves

and when my fear for her life was bigger
than my love
I released her to the steppes and flew

above it all, above the war, grasslands
snowfields, past the small horses
and the gray wolves

God in Amsterdam

The Esnoga—see time's horses
slipping down
YOUR holy walls

the 400-year-old bricks
and glass
Sabbath's opaque light

filling the women's balcony—
no service now,
just this milky glow

the Torah quiet
in its closed Ark.

'Hello, God,' I say.
'Come on out.' I know YOU
are here somewhere. After all

this is YOUR house.
The least YOU can do
is offer me a drink.

'Have a drink,'
YOU say.

YOU sit down
in the deafening rustle
of YOUR not-robes

pour good jenever into fine small glasses.
And there we are. Going at it
shot to shot. Finally

someone I can't drink
under the table.
YOU pour another,

we are jolly, YOU
answer all my questions
about death—OK—

about my own death,
about YOUR laws—I mean
are they really YOURS
or did we just make them up?
And peace—why it is so hard
—and kindness—and the dew

on the morning grasses—YOU
keep up a steady stream
of jenever—making sure

I am too drunk
to remember
YOUR answers.

Tiny Hammers

— after Psalm 37, (fragments)

I imagine YOU rooting around in me, breaking
        things
laughing YOUR holy laugh
at my pointless
        preservations
continuing to tinker
        sometimes I can feel
        the shifting. I hear tiny hammers
when I listen closely.

Today I ruined YOUR handiwork
again—
there was quiet for awhile
        then YOUR tinkering
        resumed.

I'm standing at the gates
do YOU hear me?
I set up
my finest network, my best
receivers, there is always
a signal somewhere, a bandwidth
for shelter, a wavelength.

Dead Fathers Club

— after Psalm 38

I have poor
depth perception. I can't thread
a needle, can't get through.
You crossed over
long ago.
I raise my arms
to block the next
blow. And it will come.
I predict it with this
ruined machinery;
the punishment
for remembering is
another truth.
I am the patchwork woman,
my heart a low-
grade inflammation.
my skin a dated map, mottled
record of breakage,
no guide for this dark walk
towards God or blindness.
I eat my own hands
so as not
to touch another's.

1960 — Star of David Charm Tucked In

I get caught shoplifting
at the dime store—we
are the outsiders.
They call my mother. Tommy calls

me a *kike* on Halloween.
The other kids—ghouls and ghosts
—bop girls and real bad
Elvis impersonators—they stand there
in silence, sharp

like glass—the devil's pact,
the irreversible stepping over
to muteness—me,
on the porch with

the manicured bonsai—dressed
as Queen Esther with
an empty bag—I shrink back
indoors like Saran Wrap exposed
to flames, Wonder Bread in a
child's vicious hands.

My father—he built all your
damn magnificent
waterfront homes—we Jews
just weren't allowed
to live in them.

My mother
thought she could
hide this from me.

To the Death

My husband and I had a fight today about pictures—I never like the ones of me, and that pisses him off. My negativity pisses him off. In any picture taken right now, or a few days ago, or last year, I always think I look old, or tired. But tonight, I am poring over decades of snapshots and I see that there *are* pictures I like, now, at this remove. The pictures I like are the ones where I am—not just *looking* happy, but *truly* happy, at least as far as memory serves. And yet I come back to this one. My mother and I. No idea when it was taken. Before I moved to Holland, I'm guessing—so maybe I was nineteen. Who took the picture? We both seem surprised—I look like I might strangle her. Just move that hand up a tiny bit. No, this is not a happy family picture. Read the resentment in my face, the defensiveness in hers. Yet we cling to one another. We dare the onlooker to come between us as we battle each other.

Map of May–July 1956: Living Room
with Death Notification

Some things stay with you, even as they don't.
They stay with you as they change within you.
I spent an afternoon drawing a map
of the days of my father's death. What you see
in the top left-hand corner is a homunculus home
distorted by where the blood rushes fastest,
where the wreckage is most unmanageable.
There, the crazy-quilt carpet—green, blood, gray.
At six years old I lived alone
on this carpet. I built games
around the shapes, the uneven squares of color,
the lines that one could or could not step on,
the punishments I made up for myself, creating
a kind of order. I may never be able to remember
the carpet's pattern, but I dream it.
There in the corner is the pretty pinewood
TV console, the green Bakelite phone. I haven't drawn
the ringing, I can't draw the line of light that
stretched from my umbilicus to the phone,
to the sound of it ringing. To the sound of it being
picked up. Floating off to the left, my mother's
bedroom, where you cannot see the sounds she made
because I can't draw them. How do you draw
the wail, the sounds of a wounded animal?
Of things being hurled and broken?

Bureau of Records

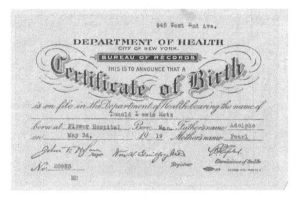

My father's birth certificate, retrieved from the endless detritus of my mother's paperwork—her mimeographs, photocopies—clogging the flow of my life's blood for nearly two decades. The beginning of a man who ended himself at age 38 rather than raise his 6-year-old child—or face his financial mess. In trouble with the law and the mafia—my mother wanting a divorce—which would have brought it all to light. But she never told me anything about this until I trapped her in a tram in Amsterdam 27 years after his death—and even then, it was piecemeal, thin, she had held it all so close for so long—it was calcified within her. Now I sometimes spend a few hours continuing to sort through her life in receipts and legal papers—whenever I can stomach it. I consign as much of it as I can to fire. My husband is the chief fire marshal—the man with the matches and his solo stove—my husband, who, in his kind curiosity—pours over it all before he lets the flames pour over it. He is the one who finds the birth certificate—I would have burned it—and that wouldn't have been the first time.

—as if YOU had them—

—after Psalm 86, verses 1–7

unable to eat enough   to feel full   or to drink enough
    to feel drunk   currently   unable to hear YOU—

    Could it be   YOUR turn   to listen?

I place these days   in YOUR hands
    —as if YOU had them—

I am keeping   a cryolog   —where I log
    all my tears   and all my waiting   for tears

—e.g. today   I almost cried   but I didn't   feel
    quite enough   —like a failed
orgasm   —so close—   but nothing.

Could YOU lift up   my heavy   listening—this unbearable
    silence   —which I have allowed—

Do YOU hear   a whisper   in YOUR
    constant night   —and then listen?

    Or just time   —which falls

apart   in YOUR hands   —as if YOU had them—

    and then   becomes   now.

God of Light and Deluge

—after Psalm 27

In the dream—the tent
above my head,
        the waters below, just enough
air between for me to sing out

and for YOU to answer?
Cup my face to YOURS?

And there it is—once I loved
        and was abandoned.

Every day we live it again, YOU and I.

And every day I swim towards YOU
        but the tides are strong.

Teach me how to crest the white waters.

YOU could just inhale me—
        keep me safe in one holy nostril
        while I wait to believe.

Amsterdam Long Window

A cocoon
a small blue egg, a chrysalis?
What does it mean
to owe someone? One night,
looking through the dark
window of the bedroom, the wind fierce,
10 on the Beaufort, true Dutch
weather, trees like ships listing
southwest, boughs wilding
no discernable pattern, one breaks under the force,
crashes through a windshield
across the street.

I see myself
reflected in the glass of our tall
bedroom window, cradling my belly, hands
new to this language
of trying to send comfort under duress
using only touch, trying
to control my signals to say—any moment
I will see him careen around the corner
on his twenty-five dollar bike, he will
come back to us windswept, boyish
and smiling. I am trying not to say—
what will we do if he doesn't? Trying not to say—
he is stubborn, I am fearful, and you
my child—I don't know you yet. I don't know
what you need.

First We Become Flesh

— after Psalm 78, verses 26–29

so fragile—such easy prey

and the wings we covet—like sand

or ashes—spread across the darkened seas.

What enters us—what is bounty—what

is threat—the answer is wrapped in time

—our construct—how we live/or die by it

crave the imagined order of it—even though

we have forgotten what it entails

to be seasonal—to wait

for harvest—to be thankful—in the season

of famine—to be grateful—even when

we are full

Messengers of Chaos

— after Psalm 78, verses 43–51

I've been thinking a lot   lately   about blood

     how sore   the overused places   of my body—my gut

       full of blood   too wounded   to drink

remember how small   she was   how I thought   she would break

     me open   and she did   afterwards there were

       green legs   beating   across the hidden path

my gut full of blood   then, too   and my labor

     my own   not now, no   now

       it is taken   I am taken   one option is

trust in the destruction   in the mystery of   next

     what is it   that is being asked   of us

       and who   asks us, who   offers weapons

the skies open   just like I did   in the new

     silence   the disconnect   of light

       my eyes are so   unused to these   shards

what am I   looking for   but messengers

of chaos   busted cups   of anger—more shards

but different   and drenched   in poison

I walk towards   a leveled path   and the path

is not   given easily   I do not

give over   easily   or meadows

of clovers, dandelions, nettles, on rare occasions,   Cowslips

here, my firstborn   arrogance   my firstborn

hate   drown them   I dare YOU.

Daughter and Mother, Amsterdam, Tram 4

Stadhouderskade

[...   ]

Frederiksplein

Did you ever miss him?

Prinsengracht

No, I was too angry.

Keizersgracht

[...   ]

Rembrandtplein

[...   ]

Spui

How did he really die?

Dam

[...   ]

Centraal Station

[...   ]

Dam

[...   ]

&

—*after Psalm 90, verses 1–7*

It is given to us to soar—which means
    witness—which means
        notice—the several birds
            their breasts & colors
                the untidy pathways—the arc
                of two trees
                    their flowering

                  if YOU are
            a verb—an interaction—
        then my fear
     frightens YOU &
   then here we are
  together & battered
by imaginary beasts

ancient & known
    & mysterious. Come, let us
        count things—like children
        do, seeking comfort,
            like the queen
              in the fairy tale
              we number

                & in the numbers
            is wisdom (some-
        where) & small animals
      & storms & time
    the length of it
   its compression
YOU & I

searching for each
    other—for the loosening
        finally, of the tight
           & stubborn chest
              (or whatever constricts
                in YOU at YOUR times
                  of constriction)
                    whatever spits YOU out

into the light—let
it spit me too—spew
me headlong into
spackled days
I promise YOU—
YOU will feel so much
better—if I can only
remember to notice

& if this is an activity
of balance—then
could YOU please
hold up YOUR end
of the fine wooden
box—the particular clouds?
Look! See how hard
it is to keep the heart

open—the focus
kind—the ledger
balanced—& can we
skip the scale
& the feather?
Climb out
of old tombs
& into new clay?

All these children
their unexpected
paths—our hearts
following, deep
in conversation
with YOU—that is
if we remember
to soar

if we remember
our hands—the wonder
of them—how we
can touch the skies,
knit together
the stars,
or so it seems
(sometimes). Amen.

Tunnel

—after Psalm 70

I begin again, step
into the long tunnel,
listen, try to catch

the memories, they shimmer
fade. I follow some,
some follow me,

and where's the harm?
It is only my urgent turning
on one lame foot.

YOU, all shadow and search
grown full
on inconsistent love, please

reel me through, catch me
on the other side
with YOUR hidden hands.

We Are All God's Poems

God, YOUR desk is vast
      —and since YOU are
           everywhere—the desk is
               —in some sense—
                  portable—
                  like the stars

I imagine YOU hitching up
      YOUR glorious robes—
           YOUR living garment
               gathering it all up—
               to sit

at YOUR desk—
      cluttered
           with notes and fragments—YOU
               are diligent—YOU show up
               to the blank
               page

every day, and today [if YOU
      have things
           like days]—well, let's call it
               'today'
               —or 'now'—

YOU are working
      from a prompt—it's
           endearing—all around YOU
               [which is everywhere]
               are scattered

tiny sparks of light—
      YOUR rough drafts
           waiting for release—longing
               for each other—and maybe a place
               at YOUR side
               [which is everywhere]

[which is everywhere]

– after Psalm 84

Inside YOUR tents [which are everywhere]
YOU are passing out first aid kits, blankets, inhalers, taking on
YOUR many forms
that we are so slow to recognize

YOU
pulling like a compass
a vortex, a tornado—
but so much stillness
and in the eye of it

the sparrow makes her nest—deposits
her young as if safe because everywhere
because nowhere and now—how fragile YOUR endless
silence—the whirr of it [which is everywhere] –
the whirr of my prayers.

If praise is what YOU need, come
and get it—but please leave the bird
in peace—her eggs—our roundness
so essential

rolling through my heart's
highways looking for signs
on how to use this strength that YOU
have provided—

enough to cross over to YOU
—the fragrant trees
I have so much to learn—the pain
YOU have provided
has honed my senses—I am here now.

YOUR rains [which are everywhere]
are harsh—I scamper
towards cover—caught
in YOUR deluge—and drenched.

—allow me
to hesitate

before I enter YOUR sun—before
I need to be mindful
and upright—let me rest
in my imperfections

let me be wet and silent
at YOUR threshold [which is everywhere]

Intaglio

As Moses was dying, we stood poised
to cross over the Jordan,
to finally enter into the land.
For forty years we had wandered
the desert wilderness.
We were tired. We wanted a home,
We just wanted to unpack.

We didn't think to ask
what we might lose,
what it would cost us to satisfy
this need for domesticity, this need
to be crated every night.

Now, we traipse back
into the wilderness
to search for God, stand
at a precipice, look
for what is unknown, unfamiliar,
uncomfortable. My husband

has turned to intaglio, looking
for that seditious discomfort,
the newness, then the slow mastery
that shifts attention away
from the tools. They fade
to transparent, YOUR hands
reach through them, and they are
briefly holy.

Doppler Effect

—*after Psalm 78, verses 9–16*

What does it mean, to turn?   Turn towards,
                                    turn away, turn tail,
turn the wood   on a lathe,   make it beautiful,
        turn as a stone   or a shell   in the darkened seas
until smooth,

        return,   turn back   to what you thought   you left behind,

come back,   smoother now,   chastised
        by your own salt,   a bit braver

This is what I mean about time,
        the false sweep of it—   the imagined flow
        what I remember—   what
                        I forget
        the small kindnesses,
                when YOU come close,   how even that

can't push it down for long—   turn
        the pain over and over
                until,   like a pearl, it grows
luminescent and regular.

And then this,   too,   is what I mean   about time
how it stops here,
                how we cast a circle
                        and YOU split me open   and something

passes through   —   or I pass through something

        as the siren passes   through the night—
everyone's emergency

eager to stop time,   to turn back—   just
for a moment—   without   turning to salt,   thirsty
    for water from the rock.

What I want   is to feel   the world
    without pulling back,   to be able
      to stretch out   my hand.

Ink,

—For Flower

the bold interpreter—300 million years
        of cephalopods
                spewing ink
        for concealment—for poison or healing
for refuge. Plumes across the depths—

which is to say; Dearest F,
        I made so many notes today
                in my mind—as if at backyard target practice;
        —aiming sloppy at the heart of it in passing
hoping that something might stick, or transfer

        but no—not without ink—

                the go-between.

                Tell me, my love

        about your ink.

Tell me about mine.

Heart to blued fingers
        to grooved paper—or wood—or canvas
                could be skin—the pygmy
        octopus glowing in the depths
disgorging a pseudomorph of ink
        —a fantastic doppelgänger—conjured
                from ejections [ejaculations]—used to mislead
        the predator.

Women at Shiva

When a mother dies
she leaves her residue—a snail's trail
across the days of her daughters—
the trails form

glittering webs
—crisscrossing
sidewalks everywhere—
cracking them

we remember the mothers
just as we forget the trails—ignore them—
skirt them—
we get on with it—

until the next mother dies—and then
we, the daughters of the dead,
are called back
into the muck of it

the pull
of loss—the vertigo shift
in generations—the startle
of aloneness—the want—

until it is our turn
to leave
that same
glistening scar

I Find This in My Mother's Effects

Strange word, *effects*—meaning: goods, possessions, personal property—usually used to indicate what a dead person has left behind—as if they had carefully sorted through their things before they died—choosing what to take with them, and what to leave behind. Imagine that. "I'll leave her the death certificate—she'll enjoy that." My mother's *effects* could also mean the mental or emotional impressions she left behind. I could have found this 17 years ago. But instead of poring over it all, I packed up the cabinets and boxes of paperwork she had so meticulously labeled and filed—labels like *Important past*—or *Do not keep.* It was wildly disorganized, like her mind in those last years. I stored the boxes. I left them closed and taped. I lacked the strength. One might ask: if this is the death certificate of my father—clearly telling me (finally) how he really died—why am I speaking of my mother? Fair question.

Wherever We Remove

There are never enough watches—I mean,
if you are ambidextrous, you certainly need at least
two if you want to know the 'hour' kind of time—the 'our' kind
of bankrupt time—you need at least
two watches to diagram your bewildered
human days—how they turtle and tank
in the fable of time.

Maybe there are never enough fathers or husbands
because they have these mysterious tendencies
to disappear—maybe time was too much
for them—too glass-bottomed, too delinquent,
shorn of promise by their own tripwire tears,
standing at home's tollbooth
with empty pockets, rancor and slippage, retreating
before the scorched earth of their own making. Maybe
we need to confiscate the timepieces altogether, all the things
that instantiate time's false swish and ripple.
Consider the calendars—lunar and solar—Zoroastrian,
Vedic, Hebrew, Greek, Roman, Islamic—because we needed
to mark our Gods, or organize our train and bus schedules,
or regiment child-feedings. There is never
enough time—and yet
we wiggle and dune it.

If Your Father Dies and Your Mother Lies

This is the only picture I have of me with my half-sister. I didn't know that I had a half-sister until I was 33. After I found her the first time, we tried to be siblings—but we weren't in the habit. It occurred to me that she was older than me—that she had known about me, but had never tried to find me. She blamed me that our father left her mother for mine, who was pregnant with me at the time. We couldn't sustain. Years later I was sitting with my friend—New York apartment—late night—wine glasses and secrets—I remembered her. My friend was mystified that I would lose touch with my only sibling—was the resentment worth the loss? It took me years to find her again. This time we were older, easier with our pasts, greedier for the future—whatever was left of it. And now, we are trying—unearthing all the bits of each other's pasts—naming things. I didn't know there was a picture of us together. But she told me that we had once met as children. She remembered because it was forbidden that we meet. She remembered because, she said, I was such a spoiled princess—I was the one who had to dress up in the only red cape—I insisted on wearing the bauble on my forehead. I haven't yet gone through all of the 20+ boxes of pictures my mother left, but I did find that one picture. That's me, the smallest, in the white dress. It's my half-sister wearing the cape and bauble.

Daughter and Mother, Amsterdam, Tram 4

Spui

But you know, I've told you.

Rembrandtplein

How did he die?

Keizersgracht
Once I surprised him at his office up in the city.

Prinsengracht

Go on.

Frederiksplein

[…   ]

Stadhouderskade
We went with a group to his favorite city restaurant.

Ceintuurbaan
The Maître D' greeted him: "Where is your wife tonight?"

Lutmastraat

[…   ]

Amstelkade
A few days later, I told him I wanted a divorce.

Victorieplein
We had dinner that night with friends.

Waalstraat
He kept saying things like: "What do you think a man should eat for his last meal?"
He was always so melodramatic. And he was drinking.

Maasstraat

[…   ]

Dintelstraat

Go on.

31

For Luz

Death blocks me, dear one—especially
the death of the father. Your father
died, and here I am—paralyzed—although

                it is you whose recent eyes
        were hollowed by that rogue, time—
            we watch it like the slow dance
        of old horses coming for sugar—no

            hurry—just want—or maybe *want*
        is too strong a word—maybe we just
                take whatever is next
        on the path—whatever presents itself

                —death, sugar—always
    on the docket—and now you, my friend—distant
        in the plague's vortex—mourning while I

    freeze & shiver in the headlights of it—trying

to choose the appropriate flowers—and my people
    don't give flowers for death—so I stand here
        stock-still in the flower market. Oh.

                This useless grief.

Poets of Blessing and Praise

—For Allison

At the time, I thought I looked old in this picture—my negativity, my husband would say—but now, only a few years later—how young we were. Today, an unusual moment of being alone—no needs more urgent than my own—earbuds in, walking Los Angeles—it's only April and already too hot at midday—listening to Monica Sok talk about how hard it is for her to write about joy. Li-Young Lee said, "My hope is that someday I will be a poet of blessing and praise. Still, I know I need to get there authentically, I need to find my real way home." And I am that poet, too—my husband raging at me last night for being negative—and yet—here we are—two poets joyous with the prospects of chocolate and art before us—New York before you were a mother, before I had recommitted to this man, before the pandemic. Everything is slippery—time and words—even images—meanings slipping like wine down my throat. I praise you, dear friend, and the joy you have built. How I miss you.

Panim el Panim

—after Psalm 89, verses 34–44

I understand something tonight—
about shame

about turning, as shame holds me,
tight it its arms—about kissing

its haggard face—how it becomes
my Janus-faced mother—stranded

on her own difficult seas that flow
into the hilt of the knife—filling its shaft

with taint —driving it
into the heart of the dinner table's

silence. To speak a truth, to write it down, even
in ink that is invisible —is to rip the membrane

between the world and me—
is to be watched by sun

and moon—is to be naked
before YOU—my crooked spine,

my breasts— perfect
and capable—larger than they seem

under this soft sweater—my thick
ankles. Help me

to understand—YOUR arm
pitching me out of YOUR nest

with YOUR erratic aim—
and there is some truth in this

and some shame—I turn, naked
in its arms—and we are face

to face. How different
YOU look at my every imagining.

Pebbles along the Labyrinth

— after Psalm 31

I listen for mercy—
    I place   pebbles

along the labyrinth— smooth

    in YOUR hand

against
    the cutting nets
              of trust

I am narrow
    in the   throat

Eyes   clenched like fists

my bones   rattle out
         my grief.

In the dream
    I am a dead boat   no sound
         still waters

only the clamor
        of time
         I choose this:
             the rasp
of dry hands
    passing me   to the next

destination   my face
       burning

the wind
    singing high   a castrato.

Earworm

—after Psalm 92, verses 1–4

A song, an earworm—a sticky
        offering
                to the holiest of days
                        —take it—

                        here
                is my attention—just YOU
        and me and this endless
song

YOUR names and names   and names
        and all this   praise
                —how hard it is
        for me to speak
of joy—to see YOU

as kind—   to think   of YOU

as faithful—could YOU
        just balance me out? Maybe lighten
                the first curse?
                        —every string

                        vibrating the same
                song—the same memory—in different
        versions—in changed
harmonies—

        The endless repetition
                of the first loss

Framework

—after Psalm 92, verses 5–9

Is it the ancient structure of song

    that decrees—tonight, I am to be

        present in the delight

            of YOUR hands?

The silences YOU

    design—patterns

        of curl and risk—of disappear—hot

            to the touch.

Clap hands—flame doused,

    dark cake—sugar

        —across years of bitter; "Here"

            YOU say—and sweet

and sometimes YOUR hands

    and sometimes my tongue—the courage

        to dip it

            into what might be

—at any moment—

    taken

Sight Reading

My mother would say 'yes' without reading
the poem, 'beauty'
without looking at me—
meaning—you are beautiful
to one who does not see you.

Perhaps *it was expedient*
that one person should die.

But when she listened, she would say
'you are rushing.' How we disoriented
each other within the measure, she
leaning her jazz
into the backbeat, her hands swift
across the keyboard, her swing

sly—lopsided against my
classical dotted 8th notes
—nearly flawless—
I practiced them for hours
in foreign countries—cold rooms,
fingerless gloves, the dragon fog
of my own breath.

Song of Songs

Time is a lion—all speed and stealth and danger—endangerment. How much of my life have I now lived without this instrument—the flute that was my world for decades? I carried it everywhere—practiced on airplanes—lay in front of heaters to warm my hands before concerts. Even after I left the stage, I played with my child at her piano. Until I didn't, until we didn't. Every once in a while, I miss it—abruptly—deeply like a thirst—I miss the pure of it— the welling up when I am truly in the music. How animal I was—how feline. Tonight is a special sabbath—the Song of Songs—we celebrate love with alluring texts—argue about why the rabbis included it in the cannon—*oh come my love*—and who is this 'love'? God is it YOU? Who are the lovers— what does it matter? I say, let the meaning shift and shimmer according to our needs. Tonight, for the first time since the pandemic, our cantor sang with other musicians in the courtyard of our synagogue—the congregation watching it online and it brought me to tears—musicians playing together again—connecting through music to each other—how it ripples out—even across these merciless ethers.

And left it in the sky

Even the small boats
are restless—they mermaid
and scoop—they are buttered—
the small boats grip the sheen
with the palms of their
small boat hands—they
are feeling overlaid, the small boats burn
the pages with their small boat
mouths—they have left so much
unsaid—they are, after all,
only small boats, and afraid
of the flames—afraid of the journey
from paper to ash—the small boats
take out their meticulously kept
notebooks—try to remember
their small boat roots—fling
their small boat windows
wide open, search
for risk. Their small boat hearts
beat light and bang and pleasure.
Their small boat lungs inhale
their own ghosts, the aroma
of blue smoke—relentless
in their trust—conjuring small
boat miracles—turning
—working
on their small boat
relationships
with YOU—

The Good Entreaty

—after Psalm 95, verses 4–11

YOURS, the deepest crevices—the light that thrusts
through me—through the earth's crust,
its mantel, its core

YOURS this territory of darkness and YOURS
the territory of light

YOURS this sullied brightness
but ours, this unholy smoke—our hands

plunging into all that YOURS have fashioned,
YOUR struggling seas—YOUR
threatened loam.

Now is the season of supplication. Now,
now is the time to crawl back
to awe.

I sometimes think I hear YOU
through the morning haze—sussurating YOUR way

through YOUR own fields—maybe plunging
YOUR hands deep into YOUR own greenery.

But more often I am trying to remember,
or not paying attention at all

And this is what I offer you—treachery—and then
turning back to YOU.

At least we have a rhythm.

Yes, I wander—I lose heart—
and then I find
my own knees again
and crawl towards YOU—[which is everywhere]

and YOU can't keep me out—no,
because now is the beseeching season—the
season of knees and craving—and YOU

have never been one to resist
a good entreaty.

Water-blind

—after Psalm 81, verses 7–11

Basket of eggs—broken, the yellow
of them flecked with promise, viscose,

and ruining my expected order—the day
as I imagined it—a slurry

of shatter. And is my heart
featherweight? The quarrel,

the test, the foolery of my own
secrets—the weight on the final

scales. I grow old, my listening
slipshod and witnessed—this fractured

testimony to YOU—my only
home—within me and yet

strange to me. This day—full of broken
and viscose and shatter—how YOU

are here—while I rummage
through my own muck—gasping,

water-blind—trying to trust enough
to open my hunger—accept

YOUR alien textures. Unlock
my uneasy throat.

Kitchen Sink

—after Psalm 96

In the kitchen, singing at the top of my lungs while the water's running, music turned up, dogs barking, I'm slicing vegetables, squeezing lemons, I'm here, in the middle of all YOUR noisy bounty

YOU bless me with this onslaught—and now I'm trying to figure out how to return the favor, how to bend to the sacred business of witnessing the day.

In every nation, drought and hunger, flood and fire, loss. Nations devouring other nations. Yet the egret, standing one-legged in the marshes, yet the sizzling of the vegetables in this pan,

yet these cities of tents and boxes, what can I do but turn and face YOUR awesome gates, and witness and witness and pour it out to YOU with heart, through my open mouth, singing at the top of my lungs?

I'm so busy with my small offices and anxious needs, while YOU make and do while I'm not looking—consider the wonders of YOUR

sanctuary, for instance, the heights of it, its windows and doors, its openings and closings, how I enter it or it enters me, then vanishes.

And then it is for me to sing YOU back to splendor, not that I have that kind of power. No, it's YOU. YOU, in your kindness, have turned up the volume.

And as I turn YOUR many names over and over, polish them to smooth stones, let me leave all these silly trinkets here with YOU.

The Green Before Her

I remember other mornings
    before she was born
        this same green—those mornings
        without—where the only darkness comes
  from within. Frosted mist rising
        over the sleeper dike. Out across the polder—for miles, nothing
            but grasses and marshlands, Godwits
        and willows, the Herons still as statues.
    Sun readying herself for dew.

Before I was mother
    all I saw in the polder
        was the *lack*—lack of music, markets,
        bookstores, concerts, crowded French-fry stands;
  no tourists bumping their roller bags along the cobblestones, taking selfies
        in front of the canals; no people busking on the Museumplein,
            no church bells' insistence, no trams clanging
        along the rails, no children
    skating on the pond in the Sarphattipark.

This morning,
    from four thousand miles away, glaciers
        on the morning skyline,
        I am holding the idea of her as lightly as I can.
  Yes, from her birth she was already moving away
        from me and into her own life, while I began the long strain,
            the pull against the mud of me, against
            that of which she was made—she, in her mercy, always
      circling back, before arcing out again, each arc wider than the last.

But it was me, wasn't it? Always
    moving away from her, steadily
        towards the abyss that will one day
        be my own.
  And then I think,
        of course, it is never just one
            body in motion, is it? If there was a light
            fading,
        it was always mine.

Legacy

In his house on the river, the man
restores broken things, for instance

the boy who is a fish, who hoards
secrets in his pockets, who shimmers

in and out of himself while the river
foams, pulling like the mad moon

on the blood beneath her, flowing
fast of late, in a hurry to show her

entrained destructions as I mumble
my morning prayers, and what recipe

for restoration could there possibly be,
I wonder, gills straining on this shore,

which was once death, and may be
death again, as we drag our children

upstream to their battered heritage.

Emerald Blue

— at Bruarfoss Waterfall

Not so cold, just rocks on the path and then
mud, uphill, trudging, bones weary, thinking

first of supper and then of whiskey, yes, perhaps
some of that even before supper, and then the sound

I don't hear at first, but rounding the bend, the dazzled
emerald blue of waterfall claims me and I remember,

for a moment, what it was like to be
loved, every part of me tender, necessary,

the water spewing secrets
under the spartan wood bridge.

I Eat My Tuna Sandwich on the Grand Canyon Rim

People stand on rocks, promontories, and ledges, sometimes
so stupidly close to the edge that I am
reminded of a book about 1000 Falls to the Death
at the Grand Canyon—

> *Awatubi Limestone, 750 million years old.*
> *Nankoweap sandstone, 900 million years old.*

They speak Chinese, German, Dutch, Spanish, French,
Hebrew, and other languages I don't recognize,
but they all make the same gesture, holding their arms
out wide, wide, facing the camera,

the Grand Canyon behind them, the gesture
universal: 'So Big' or 'My love is so big' or 'The fish
was so big.' There are hundreds of people on the trail. If
I squint just 'so' and cover my ears I can be alone. Just for a moment.

> *Cardenas basalt, 1,100 million years old*
> *Hakatai sandsone 1,180 million years old*

I am terrible at this squinting and covering. A young
boy tries to blow over the top of his water bottle to make it
moan across the canyon. As a flutist, I want to tell him:
Place the bottle just 'so' on your lips,

break your breath on the rim just 'so.' As a stranger,
I walk on in my silence, with my sandwich. People pass
along the trail, the noble panorama pushing them
to finally divulge their secrets "Mama, do you know
why I didn't want to stay in class that day…"

> *Cremation pegmatite, 1,698 million years old*
> *Horn Creek granite, 1,713 million years old.*

the secrets sweet, spoken low, girls laughing, holding
hands, touching each other's hair, the gaggle of young

French men discussing Ganesh and Krishna.
At the small promontory, a wedding in process, chanting
in an unfamiliar language. The bride in white lace

chaps, white cowboy shirt cinched at the waist, a ceremony
being led by a shaman and a deacon.
I am staring. The grandmothers, perched
on rocks with box lunches, gesture—would I like to join?
I show them my sandwich, blush.

> *Zoroaster granite, 1,740 million years old*
> *Vishnu schist, 1,745 million years old*

Two older men lost in debate on the philosophy
of the passage of time, one man's English marked
by a thick German accent, the other clearly
Israeli. A couple walks along singing
Dutch children's songs to their baby, nearly asleep
in the carrier, songs we used to sing to our daughter.

> *Brahma schist, 1,750 million years old*
> *Rama schist, 1,755 million years old*

God upon God. So many layers. One Canyon.

Daughter and Mother, Amsterdam, Tram 4

Europaplein
He didn't come home that night.

Station RAI
Two days later I got the call.

Drentepark
[　　…　　]

Station RAI
[　　…　　]

Europaplein
Yes?

Dintelstraat
[　　…　　]

Maasstraat
That he had been found dead.

Waalstraat
[　　…　　]

Victorieplein
*In a hotel. They found him because his fancy red Thunderbird
was parked for too long in the parking lot.*

Amstelkade
So then how did he die?

The Wait

— after Psalm 25

God, YOU are riddled
with caves—
all the merciful ways
of darkness

but I have
such trouble with YOUR name

what to call YOU, how
      to pronounce
            all the many
                  vowels.

                 Forgive me.
This is embarrassing.
I do choose
YOU.

        I'm listening—
        could YOU just
    reach down to me?

Here, I made this nest, full
of half-truths, I am
learning to wait for
YOU. It would be good
to wait
together.

Soundtrack

If you don't want to bring the body into this,
        and you don't, or at least that is how I
                interpret you again tonight—your reluctant hand,

on my knee—as if an animal, or an insect
        full of light and briefly synchronized
                before you lose your way in the night

although what most haunts me now is how I hear
        my own blood, how the pressure
                of flight has made my ears forget,

forget to shut out the busy sounds
        that blood makes, always moving, the faint buzzing of it,
                that our hearing learns to ignore—

the doctor explains how the body
        protects us from ourselves, our endless clamoring
                until it falters for a moment—and how

my body will eventually remember
        not to listen, in that way
                that bodies remember, will recall

the weight of your forearm
        after sex, my sleeping
                trapped beneath it, and numb.

Animal

—after Psalm 73

The dog's hunger,
the untrustworthy dream,
pacing the warrens

of our last
viable mythologies,
this is the real work

YOUR bright whispers
muffled, almost
damp, almost warm

as if YOU were mouth
against my ear.
The real work

is taming the whirring
distance between us—

Come close.

The Suicide Note I Never Received

was on creamy stationery from my father's company,
it was on smooth white paper.

It was in blue ink, it was typewritten.
He would have addressed it to me

to *my daughter, my dearest child,*
my name only, dear you. It would have

said *I loved you, I'm sorry*—
the careful words explaining

his choice to a six-year-old.
The smell of him would still linger

on the soft paper, how fragile
the pages would become after years

of being taken from their envelope,
the one addressed somehow

to me. Read and reread,
and then refolded and secured,

the envelope re-stored in secret places
wherever I went. As I grew up

the meaning would shift
even as the words

stayed the same. Imagine me
as a girl with a dead father

and my own letter. With a mother
who would never

tear that letter up, wouldn't burn it
without reading it. What

if I could remember his handwriting,
see my own alphabet in his?

The New Science of Slippery Surfaces

is revolutionizing containers.
Oil will slide through pipelines,
glue will flow, bacteria will be unable

to find purchase in stents and IV lines.
Through my one summer
as an incompetent waitress

I watched people trying to slap
ketchup out of bottles, then
use a knife. Here in the coffee shop,

I wait for you and watch
a student at the next table wrestle
with the Sriracha. And you,

my daughter, in your doctor's coat,
your wedding ring, sit down
across from me. I try not to want

too much. Consider all the ways
we try to get things out
that seem to want to stay in,

as if there were a will to it.

Obit

Metz Kills Himself; Aldon Firm Partner.

A Balboa man who was a partner in one of the nation's biggest home building firms died Tuesday in a Ventura motel, apparently a suicide victim.

He was Donald Lewis Metz, 37, of 421 M St., one of three partners in the Aldon Construction Co., 9838 E. Belmont Ave., Bellflower.

Ventura County Coroner Virgil Payton said the death was "an obvious suicide." Death was caused by an overdose of sleeping pills, Payton said. Open medicine bottles, pills, capsules and sleeping powders were found near Metz' body, the coroner said.

EIGHT SEALED letters were found in the room. Two were addressed to Metz' wife, Anita; one to a daughter, one to his mother and four to business associates. Contents of the letters were not disclosed.

One of his business partners, Willard Woodrow of Downey, said Metz had been ill.

EIGHT SEALED letters were found in the room. Two were

EIGHT SEALED letters were found in the room. Two were addressed to Metz' wife, Anita;

EIGHT SEALED letters were found in the room. Two were addressed to Metz' wife, Anita; one to a daughter, one to his

EIGHT SEALED letters were found in the room. Two were addressed to Metz' wife, Anita; one to a daughter, one to his mother and four to business

EIGHT SEALED letters were found in the room. Two were addressed to Metz' wife, Anita; one to a daughter, one to his mother and four to business associates. Contents of the letters were not disclosed.

Sometimes I think it is in the blood. You do what you can and then, one day you cancel out. The resistance falls away. 37. 70. There is no real difference. There is no real waiting. My mother was wrong, whispering to me on a tram in Amsterdam—"you're already 33. You're going to make it. We're going to be OK"—I didn't understand. But now I do. She thought if I made it to 37, I would be 'safe'. Over the threshold. Free from the family curse. But no. I didn't pass any threshold. It is always there. The door. Open.

Not like the long-disappeared envelopes, the ones that were sealed. The door is there, unsealed, sometimes barely perceptible, sometimes full and wide and vibrant. In the night, or after dinner over a drink, or in the quiet of morning. It is always there. Waiting. This morning the coffee was delicious, and the pups anointed my face in their saliva. This morning I didn't step through

Critical Care

Child, I am with you but I am not: I cannot scale the walls
you scale, your white coat, filthy
with the blood of it, the machine of need screaming
into your reverberant heart

and the dust of it, the dry winds of commodity, the savage lies of scarcity in
the angry dawn, let them find you, offer their abrupt solutions, antidotes to
the blush and shuffle of their avarice.

Or be Calypso—learn to swell out across the waters in all your unwieldy
power. Give shelter when you can, know how to take what you need, be at
peace when you must relinquish back to the insatiable seas.

                    spellbinder   oh breather

      of fire   glissading juggler

      tenacious   epiphany guardian   echo-

      locator   changeling   argus-eyed

        you—   always   listening

Sleep and wake, *neshama sheli*, sleep and wake. Be loved. Be heard. Draw down
the moon, my child, do battle with arrogance.

Be brave my love, and that is the hardest—young
and female—you speak against power—walk steady
towards the infinite need that sings to you in the soup
of your ruptured time—

This is the magic, this is the prayer,
this the seed I hurl upwards only for you.

Entre Chienne et Loup

In the hour between dog and wolf—domestic
    turns wild—and there is not enough
        light to tell them apart—
            or detect a closed door.

            Here's how to tell the difference between woman
        and pup: the pup relishes safety—the confines
    of his familiar crate—but the woman cringes
as she latches the crate door—thinks

of earthquakes, fires
    of the pup burning or buried—unable
        to exit—she feels his panic—shut in
            as she is now—wrapped in the familiar

            pattern of evenings, dog and crate—
        and perhaps that is exactly it—what she needs—
    to be up late again in her candle's light—searching
for what was once wild in her.

Hawk

Does the rabbit listen
for the hawk, and then hear him
when he flies low? Or is it this—

the rabbit hears the hawk
and then listens for distance,
for danger? Do I hear you

on the stairwell and then listen
to your gait on the stairs—infer
your mood from the cadence, the speed

or lightness of your steps?
Or do I listen for your late night
footsteps then finally

hear them? Or is it that I hear the night
cloaked in her patchwork sounds?
That they surround me,

my still and speckled eyes?
And that when I listen, the sound
of your slippers, their long chafe up

the evening stairs, will surface
like the surprise of hawk, the quickness
of rabbit—his wings, her tail.

Daughter and Mother, Amsterdam, Tram 4

Lutmastraat

[...   ]

Ceintuurbaan

Well. Apparently he had taken all kinds of pills. He'd been saving up. A full bottle
of antidepressants.
And then drank a full bottle of liquor.

Stadhouderskade

[...   ]

Frederiksplein

I didn't know he was depressed, or that he had been seeing a shrink.

Prinsengracht

[...   ]

Keizersgracht

So he killed himself? Committed suicide?

Rembrandtplein

[...   ]

Spui

Did he leave, like, a note?

Dam

Oh yes. He left me a letter. He left you a letter.

Central Station

[...   ]

Dam

What?

Spui

All this nonsense about how sorry he was. I ripped them up, threw them away.

Rembrantplein

[...   ]

[...   ]

Keizersgracht

[...   ]

[...   ]

Prinsengracht

[...   ]

[...   ]

Frederiksplein

[...   ]

[...   ]

Stadhouderskade

[...   ]

[...   ]

For My Next Trick, I Will Imagine His Death

I wish I could say: This is my final
meditation on it—for God's sake

it's been 65 years. I approach it
like a lame deer—wary

and wounded—
like the moon in motion

1.5 inches a year—but I
am moving towards rather than

in retreat—I will subsume
rather than desert, leaving the tides

to frenzy—I will heat up rather than
cool to inscrutable rock, but where

do I start? The hotel room? Or before
that—the slow collection of pills?

packing them up? Or the dinner
the night before? Or the drive—

the red Thunderbird—or the
forbidden sister? Or 4.5 billion

years ago—the moon
still close and warm. Where

do I start?

Before my father, so the story goes, planned his last supper with friends
at his favorite restaurant. I have tried to imagine the scene over and over
again. I can conjure the roast beef, fresh salad with blue cheese dressing, he
having asked her, my mother, what a man should have for his last supper,
and she, my mother, inured to his theatrics, suggesting the roast beef. I
imagine a last supper of disregarded jibes. I imagine she comes away angry.

Maybe he comes away full of resolve, maybe desperation, driving drunk, parking his red Thunderbird crooked at the motel, setting the scene that he must have walked through again and again in his mind, being a draftsman, a contractor, meticulous in his blueprints, the homes he built always beautiful to see, to walk through, placing the notes to each of us just so, taking the pills. A successful man.

Nail Polish

—after Psalm 94, verses 20–23

Wickedness and mischief—that's how
I get through my days—blood red

nail polish—I've always been
too much—always taken up space—how many

passersby have given me the side-eye—who's counting?

Not the bees—wings buzzing—looking for purchase
with their six clawed feet—their honey-basket

knees—their innocent bloodlust—letting out
their whoop-sound when startled—mostly

at night—the hive
a fortress—at its mouth, a rock—my task

to roll it away without chipping the polish—YOU
also full of mischief—always messing

with the manicure.

General Release from the Beginning of the World

GENERAL RELEASE

FOR GOOD AND VALUABLE CONSIDERATION, receipt of which is
hereby acknowledged, the undersigned, jointly and severally, do
hereby release, acquit and forever discharge ANITA METZ and her
heirs, executors, administrators and assigns of and from all
debts, demands, actions, causes of action, suits, dues, sums of
money, accounts, reckonings, bonds, specialties, covenants, con-
tracts, controversies, agreements, promises, doings, omissions,
variances, damages, extents and liabilities whatsoever, both in
law and in equity, arising out of the preparation of a Last Will
and Testament for the said ANITA METZ by the undersigned, as
attorneys at law, and arising out of the performance of any and
all legal services performed by the undersigned for the said
ANITA METZ, or for any other matter which the undersigned may
have or have had from the beginning of the world to the date of
these presents.

DATED: December 19, 1956.

ALBERT H. ALLEN
MICHAEL J. FASMAN,
a Partnership

By_____

ALBERT H. ALLEN, Individually

MICHAEL J. FASMAN, Individually

... the copy that I have was never signed. . . .

American Psalm

—after Psalm 91, verses 9–16

It's Friday—our date night. I will show up no matter how busy YOU are—I will retreat to my white couch, pull my small world in around me, warm blanket, good friends. I will do my best to be frank, and sometimes I will sense YOUR presence

OK, admittedly, YOUR presence and my ability to sense YOU—it's a Venn diagram—YOUR *oil is always slick*, YOUR *motor always running—my mirror always stained*—and us—always face to face

Oh slide and shimmy and danger—it's a trust exercise. Turn around, fall backwards into the flurry of wings

into the mosh pit of trust—the task before me is not to rebel against YOUR protection

I tell myself: Don't stumble—don't look down—even though the pebbles along the path are colorful and smooth and tempting—

I tell myself: My task is to look YOU in YOUR true face with my true face—and tell YOU everything

that I cannot tell myself—I will aspire to be merciless—and most Friday nights I will fail—I will blink, look away, flinch—

YOU will give me a whole week to repair myself—time being one of YOUR strangest gifts—and fiercest punishments

This will go on for years—

YOUR presence flickering in and out of me—a wayward filament—

For now—let's have a drink. I'll pour.

Notes

The book's epigraph is from Carl Phillips, *Then the War: And Selected Poems*, 2007–2020. New York: Farrar, Straus, and Giroux, 2022, page 22.

"To the Death" (p. 7): Pictured here is a woman with wild auburn hair and her mother.

"Bureau of Records" (p. 9): Pictured here is a copy of the father's birth certificate. Donald Lewis Metz was born May 34, 1919, in New York

"I Find This in My Mother's Effects" (p. 28): Pictured here is the photocopy of the full Certificate of Death of Donald Lewis Metz. He died on May 29, 1956. The document states clearly that his death was by suicide.

"If Your Father Dies and Your Mother Lies" (p. 30): Pictured here are four female children. The tallest is wearing a bauble on her forehead, draped over her hair with a chain, a long white dress and a long red cape. The smallest is wearing a short white dress.

"Poets of Blessing and Praise" (p. 33): The podcast was VS, hosted by Frannie Choi and Danez Smith, March 29, 2021, Monica Sok vs. Survival. The Li-Young Lee quote is taken from an interview with him that appears in *A God in the House: Poets Talk about Faith* (The Tupelo Press Lineage Series) by Ilya Kaminsky and Katherine Towler. In this picture, two women sit at a table in a chick café. Each has a glass of white wine and a piece of chocolate cake. They are smiling, heads together, into the camera.

"Song of Songs" (p. 39): The phrase in italics is paraphrased from St. John's Passion BWV 245 by Johann Sebastian Bach – which is in turn paraphrased from The Gospel According to St. John. In this picture, a girl child in long braided pigtails is playing the piano with the woman standing beside her playing a a gold flute.

"Obit" (p. 56): This is a photocopy of a newspaper article about the death of Donald Lewis Metz, stating that he was found dead in a hotel with sleeping pills and sleeping powders scattered about him, that he left eight sealed letters, including one to his daughter, and that the contents of the letters were not disclosed.

"For My Next Trick, I Will Imagine His Death" (p. 63): This picture shows what looks like a very happy young couple at the beach.

"General Release from the Beginning of the World" (p. 66): Here is a photocopy of a legal document. The document is entitled "General Release from the Beginning of the World." It releases Anita Metz, Don Metz's wife, and her progeny from any and all liability and/or debts incurred by the deceased husband.

"American Psalm" (p. 67): The phrases in italics in "American Psalm" are from Wanda Coleman's "American Sonnet 35."

Acknowledgments

To the poets who read these poems again and again, who were there at every phase, you are all champions and amazing poets. I love you. Thank you to my poetry partner, the fine poet Flower Noodle Conroy, for reading more than one version of this manuscript, for being the best editor on earth IMHO, and for being my partner in poetry crime. Thank you, Nan Cohen and Laura Hogan—poets supreme, midwives to many of these poems, who have seen almost every poem in this book, who write with me every week. I am so lucky to have you. Thank you, Allison Albino and Meghan Dunn, my New York poetry family, for your support and your brilliance. And Allison, thank you specially for showing me how family photos and documents could unleash what was trapped within. Thank you, Christian Collier, for your eloquence and always, always, your willingness to talk and to share. I approve of this. Thank you, Roy White, for sharing your fine poetry, for your patience and undying honesty about mine, and also you are so damn funny! And you, too, Crystal Stone. Dear poet, you are always there and willing to read. Thank you, Tyree Daye, for your close reading of the manuscript in an earlier form. Your input was essential. Finally, thank you to Elena Karina Byrne, who saw me early and often, for your kindness and support. Without all of you, your patience, creativity, wisdom, and your belief in me, I couldn't have made this book. I couldn't have taken the heat.

To my dear novelist friend Darcy Vebber—thank you the decades of conversation about writing, the craft, and the writing life—for the years of car rides together to Otis College of Art and Design, for dragging me to my first writer's conference. To my Psalms Sisters, Debra Linesch, Thelma Samulon, Anne Brenner, Davia Rivka, and Darcy (again), thank you for studying Psalms with me for years—one evening every week—where many of these poems started. Thank you for your openness and your intelligence and your willingness to discuss our encounters with Holiness, the sacred, our searching and prayer, and the personal and ever-shifting experience of faith.

To the teachers who woke me up, even briefly, at conferences, workshops, residencies, and formal programs, thank you. I have been so blessed to spend time with you, to have your attention on the work. Thank you, Carl Phillips, Tyree Daye, Gabriella Calvacoressi, Rick Barot, Afaa Michael Weaver, Maggie Smith, Alan Shapiro, Sarah Manguso, Brenda Hillman, Wayne Miller, Kwame Dawes, Danusha Laméris, Dennis Phillips, Paul Vangelisti, and Guy Bennet. Of course, none of this is your fault, but I couldn't have done it without you.

My poetry community has its roots in Bread Loaf. For all the years that I was privileged to attend, I am grateful. The many summers I spent there have formed me as a poet, and it is where I met so many of my closest friends and collaborators. Thanks also to these workshops and all the people who put their hearts into organizing them; Frost Place, Northwoods Writers Conference, Poets on the Coast, Napa Valley Writer's Conference and Pacific University. At each of these places, I met teachers and colleagues that still enrich my life. Thank you, also, to Dorland and Gullikistan for providing time and place to write. Thank you especially to MacDowell for giving me the time, beautiful surroundings, community, and baskets of food necessary to make poetry all day long. Finally, thank you Ross White and Noah Stetzer—for many things but especially for the Daily Grind, where many of the poems in this book were born.

Thank you, Free Verse Editions and Jon Thompson, for believing in this book, and David Blakesley for traveling with me through the formatting. Thank you and many blessings go to Brenda Hillman for singling it out.

To the ancestors and ghosts that walk with me—it hasn't been easy but I am indebted to you. For my dearest husband, Gershom, I am so grateful for your art and intelligent conversation, for encouraging me to grow and change, for supporting me on all our many journeys, for art that embellishes my book covers and the library steps you made for me. Finally, to my daughter, Mishala—you are, in so many ways, my light and inspiration. I am so lucky to have you as my child.

I am grateful to the editors of the following journals where several of these poems first appeared, at times as earlier versions:

Cultural Daily: For My Next Trick, I Will Imagine His Death
Whale Road Review: The Green Before Her
Orange Blossom Review: To the Death
Moist: Ink,

Literary Mama: Sight Reading
TAB: I Find This in My Mother's Effects
EcoTheo: Legacy
The Tahoma Literary Review: Women at Shiva
Psaltery & Lyre: God in Amsterdam, And Left it in the Sky
The Inflectionist Review: Messengers of Chaos, First We Become Flesh
Spillway: Doppler Effect
RHINO: I Need the Long March
Madness Muse Press: (which is everywhere)
→*Smartish Pace*: Tiny Hammers – (Third Place, Beullah Rose Poetry Prize)
The American Journal of Poetry: Living Room with Death Notification
→ *Los Angeles Review*: Amsterdam Long Window
→ *The Cortland Review*: Pebbles Along the Labyrinth
→ *Crab Creek Review*: Soundtrack
Pigeon Pages: Dead Fathers Club
Juked: The Wait (appeared as School Me)
→*Poetry Northwest*: The New Science of Slippery Surfaces
The Ellis Review: 1960 Star of David Charm Tucked In
Poetica: American Psalm

Star of David Charm Tucked In, The New Science of Slippery Surfaces, The Wait, and Tiny Hammers also appeared in the chapbook *Slippery Surfaces*, Finishing Line Press, 2019.

And Left it in the Sky appears in the micro-chapbook *And Haunt the World*, by Flower Conroy and Donna Spruijt-Metz, Ghost City Press, 2021

About the Author

Donna Spruijt-Metz is a poet, a psychology and public health professor at the University of California, and a recent MacDowell Fellow in poetry (September-October 2021). She attended rabbinical school for a year and a half but decided she needed to write poetry about the holy, and there are only twenty-four hours in the day. Her first career was as a classical flutist. She lived in the Netherlands for twenty-two years and translates Dutch poetry into English. Her poetry and translations appear in *Copper Nickel, Tahoma Literary Review, Los Angeles Review, RHINO, The Cortland Review, Poetry Northwest, The Inflectionist Review,* and elsewhere. Her chapbooks are *Slippery Surfaces* (Finishing Line Press) and *And Haunt the World* (a collaboration with Flower Conroy, Ghost City Press). She is on the web at https://www.donnasmetz.com/.

Photograph of the author by Alexis Rhone Fancher.
Used by permission.

Free Verse Editions

Edited by Jon Thompson

13 ways of happily by Emily Carr
& in Open, Marvel by Felicia Zamora
& there's still you thrill hour of the world to love by Aby Kaupang
Alias by Eric Pankey
At Your Feet (A Teus Pés) by Ana Cristina César, edited by Katrina
    Dodson, trans. by Brenda Hillman and Helen Hillman
Bari's Love Song by Kang Eun-Gyo, translated by Chung Eun-Gwi
Between the Twilight and the Sky by Jennie Neighbors
Blood Orbits by Ger Killeen
The Bodies by Christopher Sindt
The Book of Isaac by Aidan Semmens
The Calling by Bruce Bond
Canticle of the Night Path by Jennifer Atkinson
Child in the Road by Cindy Savett
Civil Twilight by Giles Goodland
Condominium of the Flesh by Valerio Magrelli, trans. by Clarissa Botsford
Contrapuntal by Christopher Kondrich
Country Album by James Capozzi
Cry Baby Mystic by Daniel Tiffany
The Curiosities by Brittany Perham
Current by Lisa Fishman
Day In, Day Out by Simon Smith
Dear Reader by Bruce Bond
Dismantling the Angel by Eric Pankey
Divination Machine by F. Daniel Rzicznek
Elsewhere, That Small by Monica Berlin
Empire by Tracy Zeman
Erros by Morgan Lucas Schuldt
Fifteen Seconds without Sorrow by Shim Bo-Seon, trans. by Chung Eun-
    Gwi and Brother Anthony of Taizé
The Forever Notes by Ethel Rackin
The Flying House by Dawn-Michelle Baude
General Release from the Beginning of the World by Donna Spruijt-Metz
Ghost Letters by Baba Badji
Go On by Ethel Rackin
Here City by Rick Snyder
Instances: Selected Poems by Jeongrye Choi, trans. by Brenda Hillman,
    Wayne de Fremery, & Jeongrye Choi

9 781643 173511